Dressing up as a
ROBOT

Rebekah Joy Shirley
Photography by Chris Fairclough

W
FRANKLIN WATTS
LONDON•SYDNEY

First published in 2011 by Franklin Watts

Copyright © 2011 Arcturus Publishing Limited

Franklin Watts
338 Euston Road
London NW1 3BH

Franklin Watts Australia
Level 17/207 Kent Street, Sydney, NSW 2000

Produced by Arcturus Publishing Limited,
26/27 Bickels Yard, 151–153 Bermondsey Street, London SE1 3HA

Series concept: Discovery Books Ltd., 2 College Street,
Ludlow, Shropshire, SY8 1AN
www.discoverybooks.net
Managing editor for Discovery Books: Laura Durman
Editor: Rebecca Hunter
Designer: Blink Media
Photography: Chris Fairclough

The author and photographer would like to acknowledge the following for their help in preparing this book: the staff and pupils of Chad Vale Primary School, Malachi Clearkin, Suchir Gella, Rosie Palmer-Downes.

A CIP catalogue record for this book is available from the British Library.

Dewey Decimal Classification Number: 646.4'78

ISBN 978 1 4451 0501 7

Printed in China

Franklin Watts is a division of Hachette Children's Books, an Hachette UK company.
www.hachette.co.uk

CONTENTS

Some of the projects in this book may require the use of a craft knife.
We would advise that young children are supervised by a responsible adult.

ROBODY

Robots are very powerful machines. Their power source is stored in their upper bodies.

Make your own protective casing using:

A large cardboard box (that will fit over your chest)
A pair of scissors
Coloured paints and a paintbrush
A ruler
A black marker pen
Cardboard
Gold elastic

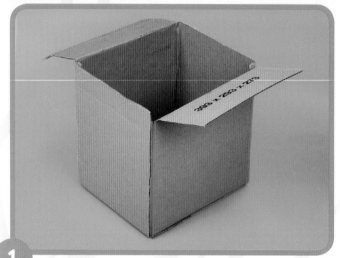

1 Open up the top of the cardboard box and cut the flaps off two opposite sides.

2 Open up the bottom of the box and paint the whole box in one colour.

3 Using a ruler and a marker pen draw diagonal lines across the box. Draw a large square on the front.

4 Paint in between the lines to make the box striped. Paint the square too.

5 Cut two oval shapes out of cardboard, approximately 12 cm long and 6 cm wide. Paint them and add some dots around the edges. These will be the robot's shoulders.

6 Ask an adult to help you make two small holes 4 cm apart on each end of the strips.

7 Make two holes in each corner of the two flaps at the top of the box.

8 Use gold elastic to **attach** the shoulders to the flaps.

Now that you've made your robot body, get ready to decorate it!

GADGETS AND GIZMOS

A robot has many different displays and dials on its body. Make a set using shiny and brightly coloured things.

You can make lots of different gadgets and swap them around using:
- Coloured card and gold paper
- A pair of scissors
- A pen or pencil
- Craft glue and a paintbrush
- Split pins
- Fun foam
- Wool and five buttons
- Velcro
- Sequins
- A ruler
- A pair of compasses

1 Cut a semicircle out of coloured card. Decorate it with strips of gold paper.

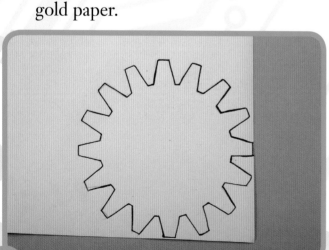

2 Draw a circle on the back of another piece of coloured card. Then draw shapes around the edge of the circle to make a cog-wheel shape.

3 Cut the cog out and decorate the coloured side with sequins.

4 Use a split pin to attach the cog to the semicircle. This allows the cog to spin around.

5 Cut a piece of fun foam into a rectangle about 15 cm x 7 cm. Ask an adult to help you make five pairs of holes in the foam. Each pair of holes should be 5 cm apart.

6 Thread buttons onto pieces of wool. Thread the wool through the holes in the foam and tie a knot at the back. The buttons will slide up and down the wool.

With your control panels and gadgets working you can get ready for some robo-action!

TIP:
Attach your gadgets to your robot's body with Velcro. Think up some other gadgets you could make and attach.

INFORMATION OVERLOAD

A robot's body has many tubes to carry wires from one part of its body to another. Lots of information is passed along these wires.

1 Cut the foam pipe in half.

TIP:

The holes should be slightly smaller than the end of the foam pipe. If the holes are too big, the pipe will not stay in place.

2 Ask an adult to cut two holes in each side of your robot's body.

3 Push the foam pipe through the holes.

4 Use a biro to make six holes in the box between the foam pipes.

5 Thread plastic craft string through the holes and tie together inside.

Now you are ready to do some serious calculations!

LIGHT ME UP

Robots often have flashing lights. They use the lights to flash warnings and coded messages to each other.

Make your robot flash using:
Two egg box bottom halves
A pair of scissors
Coloured paints and a paintbrush
Sequins
Craft glue and a paintbrush
Gold elastic
Two battery-powered bicycle lights
Four clothes pegs

1 Cut off the points inside the the egg box halves.

2 Glue the edges of the holes together to close the gaps. Hold in place with clothes pegs until the glue dries.

3 Paint the egg boxes. Decorate them with sequins and a different coloured paint.

4 Tie gold elastic around the clips at the back of the bicycle lights.

Everyone will see you coming in your robot costume now!

TIP:
Make sure that you can still reach the button to turn the lights on!

5 Attach the lights to the egg boxes by tying the gold elastic down their centres.

6 Ask an adult to help you make holes in the middle of each side of the egg boxes.

7 Thread some more gold elastic through the holes and tie around the robot's shoulders.

BRAIN POWER

A robot's head is where it receives its messages. It needs a strong **antenna** to carry information to its computer 'brain'.

Make your robot head and antenna using:
A cardboard box that will fit **snugly** over your head
Coloured paints and a paintbrush
A pair of scissors
Sequins
Coloured paper
Two egg box lids
Two plastic bottle lids
A plastic bottle
Newspaper cut into strips
Craft glue and a paintbrush
Two pipe cleaners
Two coloured drinking straws
A ruler

1 Ask an adult to help you cut out a rectangular hole in the box to make an eye-hole (about 15 cm x 7 cm). Then paint the box.

2 When the paint is dry, decorate your robot's face with sequins, paint and coloured paper.

3 Paint two egg box lids and two bottle lids. Use coloured paper, paint and sequins to decorate them.

Now you can look and think like a robot!

4 Ask an adult to cut the top off an empty plastic bottle. Then cover it with newspaper strips and glue.

5 Paint the bottle top and glue it to the top of the box. Glue the bottle lids to the egg box lids and glue onto each side of the box.

6 Thread the pipe cleaners into the straws. Bend the pipe cleaners to make an antenna shape. Insert the antenna into the plastic bottle top and glue in place.

ROBO-LEGS

A robot's body and head can be very heavy, so robots need to have strong, sturdy legs.

Make robo-legs using:
Two plastic bottles (square-based bottles if possible)
A craft knife
Masking tape
Coloured paint and a paintbrush
A hole-punch
Elastic
Two egg box bottom halves
Sequins
A pair of scissors

1 Ask an adult to cut the top and bottom off the empty plastic bottles. Then cut the bottles in half **lengthways.**

TIP: The loop of elastic should fit snugly around your leg.

2 Cover all of the edges with masking tape then paint the half-bottles.

3 Punch holes in each corner of the half-bottles. Thread elastic through the holes and knot each end.

4 Cut the points out of the egg boxes and glue the gaps (as on page 10). Then paint them and decorate with paint and sequins.

5 Make a hole in the middle at each side of the egg boxes. Thread elastic through the holes and knot to make a loop.

Now your robo-legs are ready to wear! Pull the half-tubes onto the top and bottom halves of your legs. Put the egg boxes over your knees.

WELL-ARMED

Robots are very good at doing difficult jobs. They need special, **mechanical** arms to help them to do their work.

Make your robot's arms using:

- Thin cardboard
- A pair of scissors
- An empty crisp tube
- Thick cardboard
- Craft glue and a paintbrush
- Two large plastic bottles
- A craft knife
- Masking tape
- Coloured paints and a paintbrush
- Metallic paper
- A ruler

1 Use scissors to cut three strips out of thin cardboard (2 cm by 30 cm).

2 Take an empty crisp tube and wrap two of the card strips around its middle. Glue them in place.

3 Ask an adult to cut two spanner head shapes, 15 cm wide, out of thick cardboard using a craft knife.

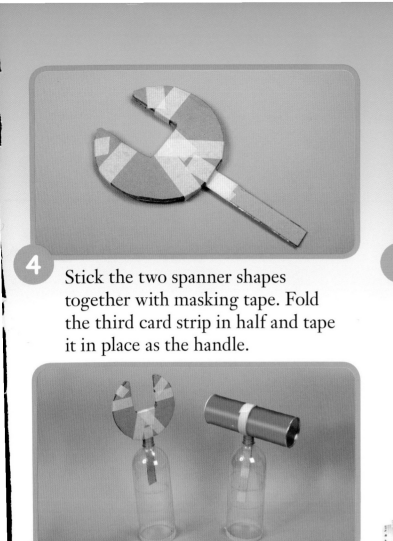

4 Stick the two spanner shapes together with masking tape. Fold the third card strip in half and tape it in place as the handle.

5 Ask an adult to cut the bottom off two plastic bottles with a craft knife. Cover the edges in masking tape.

Your robot arm tools are ready to wear. Hold on to the strips of cardboard inside the bottles.

6 Attach the spanner and hammer to the bottles by pushing the card handles into the necks of the bottles. Use masking tape to secure them.

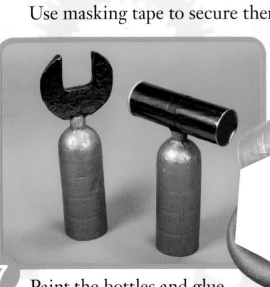

7 Paint the bottles and glue metallic paper over the hammer and spanner shapes.

BEST FOOT FORWARD

Robots wear big, clumpy shoes and move slowly but steadily in them.

1 Paint the top and sides of two empty tissue boxes.

2 Use a ruler to draw stripes around the sides of the boxes and paint stripes in.

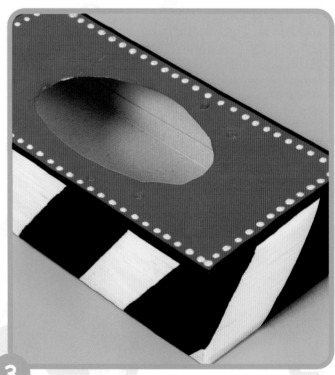

3 Add some dots of paint. Make two pairs of small holes either side of the large hole in each box.

4 Thread some elastic through the holes and tie. This will help keep the boxes on your feet.

Your robot shoes are ready to stomp around in!

THE CUTTING EDGE

A laser tool can cut through metal. This means it is useful for cutting through doors to rescue people.

1 Paint the three small boxes.

2 Glue the boxes together in a laser-like shape.

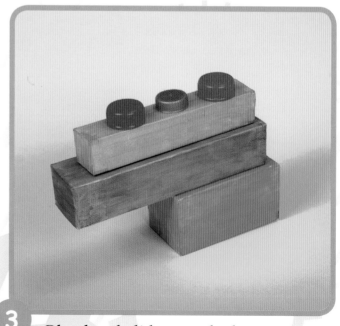

3 Glue bottle lids to make buttons on the top of your laser tool.

4 Glue a straw onto a plastic bottle lid. Then glue the lid onto the end of the laser. Decorate the laser with sequins.

Tie the laser to one of your robot arms with elastic. Your laser is ready to use whenever you need to make a quick escape!

A TIN MAN'S BEST FRIEND

A robot's life can be lonely.
So why not make a friend?

1 Ask an adult to cut the end off a plastic bottle. Cover the top end of the bottle and a box and juice carton with foil.

2 Glue the bottle top to the smaller box to make the head and nose. Glue two bottle lids above the nose to make the eyes.

3 Draw around the pipe on the bottom of the head and on the top of the large box. Ask an adult to cut out the circles to make holes.

4 Push the piece of pipe into the holes to join the head to the large box.

5 Cover the **polystyrene** balls and the card tubes in foil. Glue a medium ball and a small ball to either end of the tubes to make legs.

6 Glue two legs to each side of the body.

7 Glue the remaining balls to the ends of a 5 cm length of straw. Then glue the larger ball onto the back of the robo-puppy's body to make a tail.

Robo-Rover is ready for a walk! Perhaps you could make him a collar and lead?

GLOSSARY

antenna a wire that receives information
attach to join one thing to another
lengthways from one end to the other along the longest side
mechanical like a machine
polystyrene a white, foam-like material
snugly close fitting – but not too tight

FURTHER INFORMATION

Robots by Andy Parker (Kingfisher Books, 2010)
Stories of Robots by Russell Punter (Usborne Children's Books, 2007)
Robots Activity Book by Susan Shaw-Russell (Dover Publications, 2009)
Watch Me Draw Robots by Jickie Torres (Walter Foster Publishing, 2010)

akidsheart.com/color/robots.html
This website has lots of robot colouring pages for you to print.
funschool.kaboose.com/formula-fusion/games/game_dr_brains_robot.html
This website has a robot maths game with different levels of difficulty.
www.playkidsgames.com/games/robot/robotCalculator.htm
Use this robot calculator to practise your sums.
www.thetech.org/exhibits/online/robotics
The Tech Museum website contains lots of information about real-life robots.
www.ziggityzoom.com/activities.php?a=291
This website gives instructions on how to make a robot out of recycled materials.

INDEX